FORMING AND BREAKING COMPOUND WORDS

Reading Book 7 Year Old
Children's Reading & Writing Books

LET'S LEARN ABOUT COMPOUND WORDS!

A compound word is made by putting two words together.

Example:
cup + cake = cupcake
any + body = anybody

Complete the compound word in the sentence.

pony + tail =

back + yard =

earth + quake =

Rewrite the compound words.

Complete the compound word in the sentence.

pan + cake = _______________

lip + stick = _______________

tooth + brush = _______________

Rewrite the compound words.

Complete the compound word in the sentence.

sun   **+**   rise   **=**   __________

pop   **+**   corn   **=**   __________

after   **+**   noon   **=**   __________

Rewrite the compound words.

Complete the compound word in the sentence.

hair + cut =

____

cow + boy =

____

fire + place =

____

Rewrite the compound words.

____

Complete the compound word in the sentence.

news $+$ paper $=$ ______

foot $+$ print $=$ ______

scare $+$ crow $=$ ______

Rewrite the compound words.

Complete the compound word in the sentence.

bull + dog = __________________

hand + out = __________________

door + knob = __________________

Rewrite the compound words.

Complete the compound word in the sentence.

down + hill =

fire + fly =

cross + over =

Rewrite the compound words.

Complete the compound word in the sentence.

bed   +   bug   =

under +   arm   =

sea   +   food   =

Rewrite the compound words.

Complete the compound word in the sentence.

out + run =

wood + work =

day + time =

Rewrite the compound words.

Complete the compound word in the sentence.

ice   +   box   =   __________________

doll   +   house   =   __________________

fox   +   hole   =   __________________

Rewrite the compound words.

Complete the compound word in the sentence.

bob + cat = ...

out + door = ...

any + way = ...

Rewrite the compound words.

Complete the compound word in the sentence.

moon + light =

some + how =

sun + set =

Rewrite the compound words.

Complete the compound word in the sentence.

fire + men =

in + door =

eye + lid =

Rewrite the compound words.

Complete the compound word in the sentence.

sea   **+**   shell   **=**   __________________

rain   **+**   drop   **=**   __________________

birth   **+**   day   **=**   __________________

Rewrite the compound words.

Complete the compound word in the sentence.

mail + box =

snow + flake =

foot + ball =

Rewrite the compound words.

Complete the compound word in the sentence.

him   +   self   =   _______________

sun   +   flower   =   _______________

pass   +   port   =   _______________

Rewrite the compound words.

back + bone =

home + made =

air + port =

Rewrite the compound words.

Complete the compound word in the sentence.

spear + mint =

sea + shore =

sub + way =

Rewrite the compound words.

Complete the compound word in the sentence.

sand + stone = _______________

tooth + pick = _______________

pick + up = _______________

baby + sitter = ______________________

ham + burger = ______________________

home + town = ______________________

Complete the compound word in the sentence.

life   +   guard   =   __________

book   +   mark   =   __________

super   +   sonic   =   __________

Rewrite the compound words.

Complete the compound word in the sentence.

book + store =

key + hole =

life + line =

Rewrite the compound words.

Complete the compound word in the sentence.

fore + hand = ______________________

life + boat = ______________________

some + one = ______________________

Rewrite the compound words.

Complete the compound word in the sentence.

super + power = _______________

super + natural = _______________

water + fall = _______________

Rewrite the compound words.

watch + dog = _______________

some + day = _______________

book + worm = _______________

Rewrite the compound words.

Complete the compound word in the sentence.

back + stage = ___________________

under + age = ___________________

black + smith = ___________________

Rewrite the compound words.

Complete the compound word in the sentence.

key + board = ___________

skate + board = ___________

rattle + snake = ___________

Rewrite the compound words.

Rewrite the compound words.

Complete the compound word in the sentence.

text   +   book   =   ______________

key   +   pad   =   ______________

side   +   kick   =   ______________

Rewrite the compound words.

Complete the compound word in the sentence.

soft + ball = ____________________________

back + space = ____________________________

back + ache = ____________________________

Rewrite the compound words.

____

____

____

____

Complete the compound word in the sentence.

eye + sight = ____________________

super + hero = ____________________

day + time = ____________________

Rewrite the compound words.

____

____

____

____

Complete the compound word in the sentence.

dead + line = ___________

rain + bow = ___________

black + board = ___________

Rewrite the compound words.

Complete the compound word in the sentence.

water + melon =

black + berry =

fish + pond =

Rewrite the compound words.

Complete the compound word in the sentence.

grand + child =

note + book =

fire + ball =

Rewrite the compound words.

Complete the compound word in the sentence.

hand + made = _______________

cross + bow = _______________

slow + down = _______________

Rewrite the compound words.

____
____
____
____

Complete the compound word in the sentence.

rain   **+**   storm   **=**   _______________

candle   **+**   light   **=**   _______________

head   **+**   ache   **=**   _______________

Rewrite the compound words.

____

____

____

Write the two words that make each compound word.

snowball = _________ + _________

Rewrite the compound word.

sunfish = _________ + _________

Rewrite the compound word.

eyelash = _________ + _________

Rewrite the compound word.

Write the two words that make each compound word.

eyeglass = ______________ + ______________

Rewrite the compound word.

stoplight = ______________ + ______________

Rewrite the compound word.

pinwheel = ______________ + ______________

Rewrite the compound word.

Write the two words that make each compound word.

starfish = ______ + ______

Rewrite the compound word.

teaspoon = ______ + ______

Rewrite the compound word.

fishbowl = ______ + ______

Rewrite the compound word.

Write the two words that make each compound word.

shoelace = ___________ + ___________

Rewrite the compound word.

tablecloth = ___________ + ___________

Rewrite the compound word.

wheelchair = ___________ + ___________

Rewrite the compound word.

Write the two words that make each compound word.

tablespoon = _______ + _______

comeback = _______ + _______

teapot = _______ + _______

Write the two words that make each compound word.

wallpaper = _______ + _______

Rewrite the compound word.

goodnight = _______ + _______

Rewrite the compound word.

goodbye = _______ + _______

Rewrite the compound word.

Write the two words that make each compound word.

watercolor = _______ + _______

Rewrite the compound word.

jellyfish = _______ + _______

Rewrite the compound word.

nutcracker = _______ + _______

Rewrite the compound word.

Write the two words that make each compound word.

schoolbus = ___________ + ___________

Rewrite the compound word.

coffeemaker = ___________ + ___________

Rewrite the compound word.

scarecrow = ___________ + ___________

Rewrite the compound word.

Write the two words that make each compound word.

toolbox = _______ + _______

Rewrite the compound word.

jellybean = _______ + _______

Rewrite the compound word.

eggshell = _______ + _______

Rewrite the compound word.

Write the two words that make each compound word.

cattail = __________ + __________

Rewrite the compound word.

earring = __________ + __________

Rewrite the compound word.

typewriter = __________ + __________

Rewrite the compound word.

Write the two words that make each compound word.

matchbox =   +

Rewrite the compound word.

stopwatch =   +

Rewrite the compound word.

rubberband =   +

Rewrite the compound word.

Write the two words that make each compound word.

motorcycle = ______________ + ______________

Rewrite the compound word.

____

doorstep = ______________ + ______________

Rewrite the compound word.

____

haircut = ______________ + ______________

Rewrite the compound word.

nowhere = ______ + ______

Rewrite the compound word.

somewhere = ______ + ______

Rewrite the compound word.

passport = ______ + ______

Rewrite the compound word.

Write the two words that make each compound word.

airport = _________ + _________

grasshopper = _________ + _________

backbone = _________ + _________

Write the two words that make each compound word.

household   =   __________ + __________

toothpaste   =   __________ + __________

weekend   =   __________ + __________

Write the two words that make each compound word.

weekday = ________ + ________

Rewrite the compound word.

superstar = ________ + ________

Rewrite the compound word.

backspin = ________ + ________

Rewrite the compound word.

Write the two words that make each compound word.

superwoman = _____________ + _____________

Rewrite the compound word.

_____________________   _____________________

background = _____________ + _____________

Rewrite the compound word.

_____________________   _____________________

friendship = _____________ + _____________

Rewrite the compound word.

_____________________   _____________________

Write the two words that make each compound word.

carpool = _______________ + _______________

Rewrite the compound word.

____

____

daydream = _______________ + _______________

Rewrite the compound word.

____

____

lifesaver = _______________ + _______________

Rewrite the compound word.

____

____

Write the two words that make each compound word.

uppercut = ______________ + ______________

Rewrite the compound word.

____

grandmaster = ______________ + ______________

Rewrite the compound word.

____

caretaker = ______________ + ______________

Rewrite the compound word.

____

Write the two words that make each compound word.

cornmeal = ______________ + ______________

Rewrite the compound word.

____

highway = ______________ + ______________

Rewrite the compound word.

____

fireproof = ______________ + ______________

Rewrite the compound word.

____

Write the two words that make each compound word.

handmade = _______________ + _______________

Rewrite the compound word.

____

airline = _______________ + _______________

Rewrite the compound word.

____

schoolboy = _______________ + _______________

Rewrite the compound word.

Write the two words that make each compound word.

butternut = _____ + _____

Rewrite the compound word.

bedrock = _____ + _____

Rewrite the compound word.

headlight = _____ + _____

Rewrite the compound word.

Visit

BABY PROFESSOR
EDUCATION KIDS

www.BabyProfessorBooks.com

to download Free Baby Professor eBooks
and view our catalog of new and exciting
Children's Books